05/13

EXTREME JOBS IN EXTREME PLACES
LIFE ON AN
OIL RIG

By Drew Nelson

Gareth Stevens
Publishing

19.95 04/13

Please visit our website, www.garethstevens.com. For a free color catalog of all our high-quality books, call toll free 1-800-542-2595 or fax 1-877-542-2596.

Library of Congress Cataloging-in-Publication Data

Nelson, Drew, 1986-
        Life on an oil rig / by Drew Nelson.
cm. – (Extreme jobs in extreme places)
Includes bibliographical references and index.
Summary: This book describes how offshore drilling platforms are assembled,
some of the jobs on an offshore drilling platform, what life is like for those living on an offshore drilling
platform, and more.
Contents: What is an offshore oil rig? – History of offshore drilling – Man-made
islands – Other types of offshore rigs – Different rig jobs – Danger! – Safe and sound – In case of
emergency – Happy holidays – If you're looking for extreme
ISBN 978-1-4339-8498-3 (pbk.)
ISBN 978-1-4339-8499-0 (6-pack)
ISBN 978-1-4339-8497-6 (hard bound) –
        1. Offshore oil well drilling—Juvenile literature   [1. Offshore oil well drilling   2. Oil well drilling]
I. Title
                2013
622/.33819—dc23

First Edition

Published in 2013 by
Gareth Stevens Publishing
111 East 14th Street, Suite 349
New York, NY 10003

Designer: Andrea Davison-Bartolotta
Editor: Therese M. Shea

Photo credits: Cover, p. 1 Gandee Vasan/Stone+/Getty Images; p. 4 © iStockphoto.com/LiciaR; p. 5 iStockphoto/Thinkstock; p. 6 General Photographic Agency/Getty Images; p. 7 Shel Hershorn/Hulton Archive/Getty Images; p. 8 am70/Shutterstock.com; pp. 9, 24 Rich Press/Bloomberg via Getty Images; p. 10 © iStockphoto.com/landbysea; p. 11 Douglas Engle/Bloomberg via Getty Images; p. 11 (inset) Bob Thomason/Stone/Getty Images; p. 12 Stephen Hilger/Bloomberg via Getty Images; p. 13 (top) Leong Yoke Shu/Shutterstock.com; p. 13 (bottom) suwatpo/Shutterstock.com; p. 14 Ingram Publishing/Thinkstock; p. 15 James Wells/Stone/Getty Images; p. 16 Jerome Sessini/Getty Images; p. 17 Stockbyte/Thinkstock; p. 18 Fedor Kondratenko/Shutterstock.com; p. 19 Christopher Pillitz/The Image Bank/Getty Images; p. 20 Mark Ralston/AFP/Getty Images; p. 21 Photodisc/Thinkstock; p. 23 Alexander Zemlianichenko Jr./Bloomberg via Getty Images; p. 25 (both) Derick E. Hingle/Bloomberg via Getty Images; p. 26 Stewart Charles Cohen/ Digital Vision/Getty Images; p. 27 Andrew Bosch/Miami Herald/MCT via Getty Images; p. 28 Atta Kenare/ AFP/Getty Images; p. 29 Tad Denson/Shutterstock.com.

Printed in the United States of America

CPSIA compliance information: Batch #CW13GS: For further information contact Gareth Stevens, New York, New York at 1-800-542-2595.

CONTENTS

Words in the glossary appear in **bold** type the first time they are used in the text.

WHAT IS AN OFFSHORE OIL RIG?

In 2011, oil companies in the United States produced about 5.7 million barrels of crude oil per day! Crude oil is turned into fuel that runs cars, heats homes, and provides power for many other things. A lot of this oil comes from offshore oil rigs.

An oil rig is actually a piece of machinery that's used for drilling oil both onshore and offshore. But many people call the whole structure around the drill an oil rig. Offshore oil rigs—also called oil platforms—are home to some of the most extreme jobs in the world.

WHERE ARE OFFSHORE OIL RIGS?

In the United States, offshore oil rigs are found in a few different places. These include waters near California and in the Gulf of Mexico near Florida, Texas, Mississippi, Louisiana, and Alabama. China, the United Kingdom, and many nations in the Middle East also have large numbers of offshore oil rigs.

4

Offshore oil rigs often have many levels, somewhat like the many stories of a tall apartment building.

5

HISTORY OF OFFSHORE DRILLING

Offshore oil rigs were first **designed** almost 150 years ago. In 1869, a man named T. F. Rowland got a **patent** for the first offshore drilling platform. It was made to work in very shallow water, but it looked similar to many current models. The whole structure was supported by four legs that reached down to the ocean floor.

In 1947, the first offshore rig so far out that it couldn't be seen from shore was built in the Gulf of Mexico. Since then, oil rigs have been constructed offshore all around the world.

TYPES OF RIGS

There are two main types of offshore drilling rigs: moveable and **permanent**. Moveable offshore drilling rigs are mostly used to find oil. If the **deposit** is thought to be very large, a permanent platform is built over the well. Permanent rigs are more expensive than moveable rigs, so companies make sure the deposit is worth it.

▲ onshore oil rig

The drills on an offshore rig are much the same as those used for onshore rigs.

MAN-MADE ISLANDS

Permanent offshore oil rigs have everything the workers need to live on board for months at a time. Most of the space on a platform is taken up by **equipment** such as the drills and pumps that bring the oil out of the ground. There are also offices where computers monitor the drilling and where records are kept.

The rest of the space is for the workers. There are small living areas, places for visitors to stay, a cafeteria, and a kitchen (or galley). All rigs are different, but some might have a restaurant, a coffeehouse, a gym—or even a movie theater!

DIFFERENT SHAPES AND SIZES

Oil rigs come in different shapes and sizes. Some are small, especially if they don't have to drill deep or carry much oil. Some platforms are larger than a football field and as tall as a skyscraper. BP's Holstein deepwater platform is taller than the Eiffel Tower in Paris, France!

drill bit ▶

This worker checks the computers in the control room of an oil platform in the Atlantic Ocean near Brazil.

How do oil platforms get out in the middle of the ocean? First, pieces of the platform are built onshore. Then, each piece is loaded onto a ship and taken out to where it will be placed in the water. Sometimes these pieces are put together before—or even while—they're being transported. However, usually everything is put together once the ship or ships get to the platform's location.

Some rigs are fixed platforms, which means they're attached to the ocean floor. Their underwater pieces are put in place first. Other rigs are kept in place by anchors. Sometimes the ocean floor is just too deep for legs.

ALL-SPARS

Spar platforms are offshore oil rigs built to drill at the deepest depths. Among the largest platforms, spars have a concrete **cylinder** that reaches down deep into the ocean. The cylinder is attached to the ocean floor by cables. Spars can drill in water up to 10,000 feet (3,048 m) deep!

boats transporting oil platform

Some of the construction work on this oil platform takes place onshore. Later, it will be completed in the Atlantic Ocean.

11

OTHER TYPES OF OFFSHORE RIGS

Besides offshore oil platforms, other structures are used for drilling underwater. Drilling barges are towed to a location and left floating on the surface. They're used in shallow, still waters that won't move the barge much. Jack-up rigs are like drilling barges, except once they're in position, three or four legs are lowered to the ocean floor to hold them in place.

Drill ships are large boats capable of both drilling into the ocean floor and transporting oil back to land. Drill ships have a system of motors and computers that keep them in place over an oil deposit.

THE DRILLING TEMPLATE

Before drilling, a crew first installs a template, somewhat like a large metal box, on the ocean floor. It's put in place over a deposit of oil using GPS (global positioning system). The template guides the drill. A blowout preventer is also put in place. It keeps oil from escaping into the water.

▶ blowout preventer

12

drill ship

The type of offshore oil rig used often depends on the location and the amount of oil in a deposit.

jack-up rig

13

DIFFERENT RIG JOBS

There are many different jobs that keep an offshore oil rig working. Roustabouts are people who live on the oil rig and do a bit of everything. They repair drill parts, check pumps, and also do simple but necessary jobs like painting and cleaning.

After working as a roustabout, people move up to become roughnecks. Roughnecks do much of the actual drilling work. They also put the drills together and replace parts. Roughnecks make sure the drills operate correctly and sometimes climb into giant holes with the equipment to figure out the problem!

Both roustabouts and roughnecks work long hours and in rain, wind, and snow.

BRAVING THE ELEMENTS

Many permanent oil platforms are built in places where the weather conditions can be very rough. One location is the North Sea, east of England. Platforms there are built to withstand wind speeds of more than 100 miles (160 km) per hour and waves up to 60 feet (18 m) tall!

15

While roustabouts and roughnecks work on the deck and do most of the physical work that goes into oil drilling, other kinds of workers are needed as well.

Drillers **supervise** the roughnecks and the drilling process. They also give out daily assignments to other workers. Engineers work on **mechanical** parts of the platform both above and under the water. Electricians make sure the electrical power on the rig is working well, and mechanics work with all the machines. **Medics** are also on hand to care for sick or hurt workers when needed.

IT'S NOT ALL ROUGH

What do oil-rig workers do in their spare time? Many platforms have television so workers can watch TV shows just like people onshore do. Most also have Internet so crewmembers can read news and communicate online. Some platforms allow people to have visitors, so they might spend time with their friends or family.

Oil-rig workers can work many different shifts, including early in the morning and overnight. Many shifts are as long as 12 hours!

17

When workers on offshore oil rigs aren't working or resting, they're eating. And even though they're out in the middle of the ocean, they eat more than just fish.

Yet another job on an oil rig—and an important one—is the cook. The cook makes four to six meals a day since workers have different shifts and schedules. They make the same meals that workers get on land. But if storms keep supplies from being delivered to the rig, cooks have to get creative with their meals. Sometimes, though, they grill steaks out on the deck!

PARTY OF HOW MANY?

Cooks may have their hands full working on a large rig. Just like the platforms themselves, the crews that operate each offshore oil rig can be different sizes. Smaller platforms have smaller crews, and large platforms have crews of more than 100. That's a lot of mouths to feed!

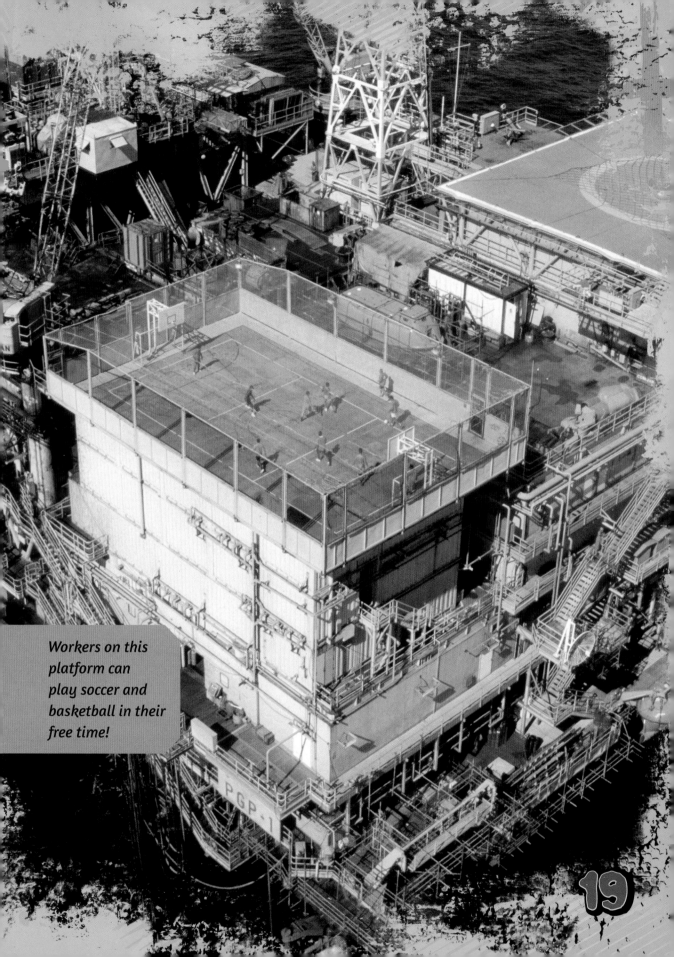

Workers on this platform can play soccer and basketball in their free time!

DANGER!

There are many dangers on an offshore oil rig. On parts of the deck, only a floor grate keeps workers from falling into the ocean. Cranes swing heavy pieces of equipment across the deck. Many drilling tools are sharp and powerful and could hurt a worker if not used carefully.

An oil well can also have a blowout, which is an uncontrolled release of oil that flows up and out of the well. And almost everything on the platform has oil or gasoline on it or in it. This can make many things on the platform quickly catch fire or even explode.

FINDING NEMO

At times, it might seem like crews on offshore oil rigs are living in small cities separate from nature. However, workers can actually see sea creatures in the ocean! On rigs in the Gulf of Mexico, workers often see manta rays, sharks, and bluefin tuna swimming below.

This worker helps direct a huge crane used for lifting equipment on an offshore oil platform.

21

SAFE AND SOUND

Because of the many dangers, safety is a major concern on oil platforms. Several measures are usually in place to help keep everyone safe. People working on the platform wear safety hats, protective clothing, and plastic glasses.

Workers have to deal with extremely loud noises coming from the machines as well as blowing winds. They often can't hear others yelling to them. Safety signs are located around every part of the deck. Even though the workers have been trained, it's good for them to have reminders to be safe. They practice **emergency** drills every day.

TURN IT DOWN!

There are many differences between working on an oil platform and working at other places onshore. One of these is the constant loud noise all day and all night. **Generators** run electricity, drills whir, and cranes drop pieces of metal. It's no surprise crews always wear earplugs!

Workers carefully fit drill pieces together on an oil rig near Russia.

23

IN CASE OF EMERGENCY

With all the dangers that exist on an oil platform, there's always the chance there will be an emergency situation, such as a fire or a strong storm. Even though crews perform drills to prepare for these, there's actually very little they can do to get away.

Most platforms have escape pods, which are like lifeboats. Workers get into pods and are lowered into the ocean. They float on the water until help arrives. When a platform is many miles away from shore, the crew might have to wait in the pods for hours before they're rescued.

COMING AND GOING

When crewmembers aren't working, they might leave the platform and go to the mainland. This depends on their assignments, how far the platform is from shore, and how much time they have. Workers may go to shore by helicopter or boat and spend the day before coming back to work.

This platform has a helicopter pad and escape pods to transport workers in case of an emergency.

escape pods

HAPPY HOLIDAYS

Besides working long shifts, many people on offshore oil rigs work overnight, too. The drill must operate 24 hours a day, 7 days a week, so someone always needs to be watching the equipment.

Many employees work these long and late shifts for 2 or 3 weeks at a time. After those weeks, they get about 3 weeks off so they can go back to shore. This means that oil-rig employees don't work about 60 percent of the year. Some workers spend this time with their families onshore.

WORK HARD, REST HARD

Working long shifts on an oil rig can be dangerous, too. Tired workers can make mistakes. So after they finish their shift—even if it was 12 hours long—they get the same amount of time to rest. This way, they'll be fresh for their next shift and ready to work safely.

Some workers have to prove they're physically fit before they even get the job!

27

IF YOU'RE LOOKING FOR EXTREME...

Life on an offshore oil rig is extreme. The work is hard and dangerous, the hours are long, and the living takes some getting used to. But many people love it! They choose to go out on the open water for the good pay and many vacation days.

Many oil-rig jobs don't require special education. For example, roustabouts and roughnecks learn on the job. Engineers and mechanics need advanced education, though. Everyone who wants to work on an oil rig has to be strong, smart, and ready to live in extreme conditions!

▲ offshore platforms in the Persian Gulf

THE TALLEST

Although many offshore oil-drilling platforms are very tall, one towers above the rest. The company Chevron built Petronius, the world's largest oil platform, in the Gulf of Mexico. Not only is it the biggest rig, but it's one of the tallest freestanding structures in the world at 2,001 feet (610 m)!

This oil platform, called the Devil's Tower, is located in the Gulf of Mexico. It can produce 60,000 barrels of oil in a day.

GLOSSARY

cylinder: a long, tube-shaped object

deposit: an underground supply of oil

design: to create the shape or pattern of something

emergency: an unexpected situation that needs quick action

equipment: tools used for doing certain jobs

generator: a machine that uses moving parts to produce electrical energy

mechanical: having to do with machines

medic: one who treats people when they're sick or injured

patent: a writing from the government recognizing something as the property or idea of the owner

permanent: meant to last or stay in place for a long time

supervise: to watch over

FOR MORE INFORMATION

Books

Farndon, John. *Oil*. New York, NY: DK, 2007.

Landau, Elaine. *Oil Spill! Disaster in the Gulf of Mexico*. Minneapolis, MN: Millbrook Press, 2011.

Thomas, William David. *Oil Rig Worker*. New York, NY: Marshall Cavendish Benchmark, 2010.

Websites

How Oil Drilling Works
science.howstuffworks.com/environmental/energy/oil-drilling.htm
Read a detailed explanation about how oil drilling works.

Oil, Gas, and Geothermal
www.consrv.ca.gov/dog/kids_teachers/Pages/
Learn more about oil rigs and different kinds of natural energy resources.

INDEX